SEASONS

Kelly Dykstra

Thrill & Move Worldwide
St. Paul, Minnesota 55101

SEASONS: A 14-Day Devotional
Copyright © 2018 by Kelly Dykstra

Cover design & editing by Tracy Keech

ISBN-13: 978-0-9960223-6-1

DEDICATION

About 20 years ago, when I was a young wife and mother,
just starting out, I got a pizza stone.
Like me, that stone was new to its purpose in life. It started out
a fresh, light beige color. Sometimes, baking pizza or cookies
would stick to the fresh, new, porous surface.

Over the years, with much use and lots of really high heat, that
stone has changed a great deal. It's now a rich golden
brown, with deep color variations where countless chocolate
chips have melted, sugar has caramelized,
and cheese has toasted.

Nothing sticks to it anymore. It is seasoned.

Over the years, through much use and the (sometimes
uncomfortable) heat of experiences, people, opportunities,
failures and victories, I, like my pizza stone,
have changed a great deal.

Stuff doesn't stick to me so much anymore.
I'm a little more seasoned.

This little book comes with a tip of my hat to each person
who has been a part of my seasoning.

Ecclesiastes 3:1-13

To everything there is a season,
A time for every purpose under heaven:

A time to be born,
And a time to die;
A time to plant,
And a time to pluck what is planted;

A time to kill,
And a time to heal;
A time to break down,
And a time to build up;

A time to weep,
And a time to laugh;
A time to mourn,
And a time to dance;

A time to cast away stones,
And a time to gather stones;
A time to embrace,
And a time to refrain from embracing;

A time to gain,
And a time to lose;
A time to keep,
And a time to throw away;

A time to tear,
And a time to sew;
A time to keep silence,
And a time to speak;

A time to love,
And a time to hate;
A time of war,
And a time of peace.

What profit has the worker from that in which he labors?
I have seen the God-given task with which
the sons of men are to be occupied.
He has made everything beautiful in its time.

Also He has put eternity in their hearts,
except that no one can find out the work that
God does from beginning to end.

I know that nothing is better for them than to rejoice,
and to do good in their lives,
and also that every man should eat and drink and
enjoy the good of all his labor—it is the gift of God.

INTRODUCTION

To everything there is a season,
A time for every purpose under heaven.
Ecclesiastes 3:1

To everything there is a season.

When I was a young mother laboring in a haze of diapers, laundry, chicken nuggets, coupons, bills, sleep deprivation, and sticky floors, my mother said to me, *this too shall pass.*

Sweet of you to say that, Mom, but I highly doubt it. I thought potty training would never end. I was destined to spend the entire rest of my life camped outside my daughter's bedroom door to train her to stay in her big-girl bed at naptime.

And then I blinked.

Kid number one just got married. Kid two just inherited her dad's old truck and took off for the summer, kid three is applying for jobs the minute he turns sixteen (tomorrow!) and the search for 50-cents-off coupons has morphed into college-financial-aid-applications.

Friends I thought were forever are no longer in my Contacts. Things I thought mattered don't anymore. I've loved and lost and learned and lived, and along the way, I've discovered that every season ends and morphs into a new one.

And the more seasons I experience through the grace of God, the more *seasoned* I become.

This too shall pass. Happy, sad, boring, confusing, stressful, painful, beautiful.

It is just a season, and seasons change.

Each day for the next two weeks, I'll meet you here to walk though the first part of Ecclesiastes 3, where we read of the push and pull of the seasons of life. For each day, you'll have a chance to jot down which of these seasons you find yourself in right now.

My hope and prayer is that this time will help you see that where you are isn't where you'll be a year from now, and that's good. God is scheming up some sweet times with you as He walks you through this season, and the next, and the next…

He has made everything beautiful in its time.

DAY 1

A time to be born,
And a time to die.
Ecclesiastes 3:2

You didn't choose your natural birth. It just kinda happened to you, and you were just along for the ride. Psalm 139 talks about God and you, just the two of you, in the dark place where you were formed. It tells how He created you uniquely *you* in a purposeful, thoughtful, secret fashion known only to Him. It tells how He knows every teensy aspect of you and your life.

If He was that intimately involved in your formation, wouldn't you think He'd want to be intimately involved in all the seasons of your whole life?

It's fitting that we start with birth, because the Creator of our seasons calls us to a *new birth* into life with Him. A spirit-birth where the *real you* comes to life in Christ Jesus.

Jesus died to give us the opportunity to be born into a true, deep, rich life hand-in-hand with God our Creator. What we see – the natural world – is only a season. God is timeless, and Scripture says that He wants to spend forever with you. This life does not end when earthly death comes.

For you have been born again, but not to a life that will quickly end. Your new life will last forever because it comes from the eternal, living word of God. As the Scriptures say, "People are like grass; their beauty is like a flower in the field. The grass withers and the flower fades. But the word of the Lord remains forever." 1 Peter 1:23-25 (NLT)

There's a time to be born, and a time to die. You couldn't choose your natural birth, but you *can* choose your spiritual birth.

When you're born into God's family, you are welcomed into a relationship with your Creator. He protects you, provides for you, pursues your heart, and will not leave you to weather any season alone. You are born to the life He dreams for you. That's what a spiritual birth does.

At the same time, a death happens. You die to your old life. You know, the one where you were fully responsible for yourself, with all the pressure and stress, confusion and loneliness. Where you wondered if it would ever get easier or better, and whether there was any purpose in your pain.

Birth. Death.

Today could be your day for both.

Will you choose to be born to meaningful, purposeful, abundant life in Christ? God will take your hand and walk you through your seasons of life. You will have His Word (the Bible) to equip you, His Mind (Holy Spirit) to direct you, and

His family (the Church) to do life with you.

Will you choose to die to your old life that held no clear answers, a continual cycle of trial and error, and a vague hope that it will all turn out in the end?

Simply pray this prayer aloud from your heart:

Dear God,

Please forgive me for where I've gone wrong and missed Your best for me. I believe that Jesus died to pay for my sins and give me new life in Your family. Today I choose to be born into this new life, and I choose to die to my old way of doing things apart from You. Please lead me through each season of my life. I will follow You.

In Jesus' name I pray, amen.

***

BIRTH CERTIFICATE

This hereby certifies that I, _____,
have been re-born spiritually. Because of Jesus, from this day forward, I have the Holy Spirit of God guiding me and walking with me through the seasons of my life. I die to my old life and am a born member of God's family, with all its privileges and benefits.

_____   _____

Signature   Date

DAY 2

Do you ever feel like you did the right thing, but you aren't reaping the benefits?

You started going to the gym or stopped eating Oreos in bed, but the scale hasn't changed.

You decided to stop nagging and start praying, but your husband still leaves blobs of toothpaste in the sink.

You began to tithe, giving God His part of your income, but money still seems so tight.

You chose sobriety a week ago, but blew it yesterday.

You memorized the Bible verse that was supposed to help you stay calm, but you still find yourself freaking out.

You are not alone. I'm right there with you.

How about this: Think of doing the right thing as planting little seeds that will grow into the life God has for you.

Close your eyes and imagine that prayer for your husband like a little seed you're planting in the ground and covering with some dirt. I'll wait while you imagine it.

Got the image? OK. Now look back at your seed. Can you see it? No. Why? It's under the dirt. Because it's planted. Your part with that little seed is done. Now what do you have to do?

Wait.

Waaaaaaaaaaaait.

Why? Because seeds take time to sprout and grow. And while they're doing their thing in the darkness, the only one who can monitor and nurture their progress is… you guessed it… God.

What do you do in the meantime? Well, if you want more harvest, you keep on planting seeds. Every time you choose to do the right thing (even if you don't see results), you are developing the skill of doing the right thing.

There is a time to plant, and a time to pluck what is planted.

If you know the right thing to do, keep on doing it. You're in planting season!

And let us not grow weary while doing good, for in due season we shall reap if we do not lose heart.
Galatians 6:9 (NKJV)

God promises that when you do good, you WILL reap the benefits "in due season" – in pluck-what-is-planted season, if you do not lose your heart for the doing.

One day, out of the corner of your eye, you'll notice something different. You'll look closer and realize something has changed! That area of your life has grown... and there's – what?! – there's fruit! You'll examine it and realize that while you just kept focused on your planting, God was focused on the growing. And then, fruit for you!

As I write this, it occurs to me that this planting business sounds like it's optional. Like, *hey, you could plant some more good if you wanna.*

But here's a sobering verse from Scripture.

Remember, it is sin to know what you ought to do and then not do it. James 4:17 (NLT)

As a child of God, with His Holy Spirit serving as your internal Guide, if you know in your heart the good you should do and choose to not do it, it is a sin. The word *sin* means *to miss the mark.* I don't know about you, but I don't want to miss what God has for me during this short season of life I get to live.

Here's a question for you to answer today: What have you quit planting because you've simply lost heart? Why don't you have a chat with God about it right now? Ask Him to inspire you to keep doing the right thing during this season.

***

Dear God,

I know the right thing to do is _____

_____ .

I have lost heart and given up because I didn't see results. Today I commit to keep planting seeds by doing the right thing.

Please strengthen my heart and give me hope that one day I will be able to harvest the benefits of the seeds I plant during this season.

Love,

_____

DAY 3

A time to kill,
And a time to heal.
Ecclesiastes 3:3

A time to kill. Man, there are so many places to go with this verse, but since we're focusing on what this chapter means in terms of seasons of our life, here's what it brought to mind.

Therefore, dear brothers and sisters, you have no obligation to do what your sinful nature urges you to do. For if you live by its dictates, you will die. But if through the power of the Spirit you put to death the deeds of your sinful nature, you will live. For all who are led by the Spirit of God are children of God. Romans 8:12-14 (NLT)

Do you ever think/say/do something, while it feels SO RIGHT in the moment, but about two hours later you're like, *WHYYYYYY did I do that?* Or, if you're like me, *Why did I do that AGAIN??!!*

Sometimes that old sinful nature, the one that died when we were born into new life in Christ, tries to rear its ugly head. The dumb thing is that when we DO jack things up, then it messes with our minds.

Thoughts swirl around...

Maybe I'm not really a better person. Maybe Jesus isn't really changing me. I'll never really change. It was a dumb idea to think I could live free and happy. I am just a guilty sinner, and I can't do any better.

We call these *mind monsters*. It's a typical ploy of the enemy (Satan) to get us to miss what God has for us. These verses in Romans remind us that we have *no obligation* to sin. If you fall for the mind tricks, you'll kill off what God wants to do in your life.

Instead, if you kill off what the enemy tries to do, you'll live to what God has for you!

There is a time to kill. Kill off what keeps you from living in freedom and life. A recurring habit. A way of thinking that spirals you downward. Kill off the lies. Blow up the road you keep walking down that leads you to regret.

What urge do you battle that you know is not from God?

_____

Today's the day to kill it off.

Here's a prayer to get you started:

Dear God,

I am sorry for _____.

I know my urge to do this is not from You. In Jesus' powerful name, I reject the enemy's ploy to destroy me in this area. I ask you, Father, to put to death this yucky impulse and strengthen my ability to stand firm and do the right thing instead.

Holy Spirit, please lead me in a healthier, God-blessed way to live.

In Jesus' name,

Amen.

That's a GREAT place to start. Now here's the second part: A time to heal.

When someone has surgery to remove a tumor, they don't just jump up and say, GREAT! That's over! On with life! No, there's a necessary time for healing. Surgery is traumatic on the body because it upsets what has become the status quo. Even a life-saving operation requires time for the body to heal.

Therefore, when you ask God to kill off and remove a habit or a struggle that has lived in you like a tumor, care must be taken to heal up. You'll need protection from further infection. This is a season when it's imperative that you surround yourself with Spirit-led people and stay out of environments that could lead you back into temptation.

Ideas:
Is your issue a person on Facebook? Unfriend or block them.
Anger? Consider changing the voices you're listening to. (Music, talk shows, gossip, etc.)
Drinking? Dump it and don't go to the bar.
Bitterness? Ask a spiritual leader to pray with you about forgiving and letting go.

Anxious/depressed thoughts? Google Bible verses for peace, write them down, and post them around your house.

Addiction? Find a meeting and get a sponsor.

Food issues? Make a plan for what you'll eat and when.

Marriage resentments? Try talking with a wise, godly couple or going to counseling.

A time to heal. It's a season that must be intentional. Protect yourself as you lean into God and ask Him to renew your mind and body and spirit so you will *live*.

***

What is your action step today to begin the season of healing?

DAY 4

A time to break down,
And a time to build up.
Ecclesiastes 3:3

Break it down.

I can't help it. I hear those words in MC Hammer's voice in my mind, singing *U Can't Touch This*. Anyone else remember 1990? Yes? No?

It doesn't matter. That has absolutely nothing to do with today's conversation.

Anyway. A time to break down, and a time to build up. The words *build up* bring to mind a verse in Proverbs that has inspired me over the years.

A wise woman builds her home, but a foolish woman tears it down with her own hands. Proverbs 14:1 (NLT)

This verse has always served to remind me that when it comes to caring for my home, I am either building it up, making it better, more functional/cozy/livable/welcoming, or I am letting it go, and by my lack of care, it is getting run down.

A wise woman builds up, improves, her environment. There's a season, according to today's verse, for building up, but there's also a season for breaking down.

In the context of running a household, I find there occasionally needs to be a season of breaking [it] down. Think for a minute: what bugs you about the way your household runs?

The place everyone dumps their stuff right inside the door?
How no one cleans the lint trap in the dryer?
The junk drawer?
The fact that you can never remember which week is recycling pick-up?
The overflowing trash can in your kid's bedroom?
The fact that no one can ever find _____?
The perpetual mountain of clean laundry that needs folding?
The giant pile of dishes in your way when you start to cook dinner? (That's mine.)

What bugs you? _____

Maybe you need a whole separate sheet of paper. No judgment here.

Now, break it down, Hammer-style. Ask *why.*

Why does this thing happen? Does the lint trap not get cleaned because there's no place to toss the lint? Is there a junk drawer because no one knows where those items should go? Does your kid just need a larger trash can? Do you need to make a plan to watch TV for a few minutes while you fold laundry so you don't hate it so much? (Me.) Have you never given your family a tour of the kitchen so they know where stuff should go?

Every couple of weeks after we moved into our new house last fall, I would yell, "WHERE IS MY MEAT THERMOMETER? WHERE IS MY MEAT THERMOMETER?" I'd be trying to cook dinner and get super frustrated because I had never trained my kiddos to put it in the drawer by the stove.

Yesterday I was asking my son Aidan to *please* start dealing with the breakfast and lunch dishes earlier so I can make supper in a clean kitchen. He said, "Mom, we need to create a better system."

A time to break down. When you have a calm, clear mind (like right now, maybe, and not when you're in the middle of get-food-on-the-table-so-you-can-get-to-soccer-practice), take a minute to identify where you simply need to systemize a better functionality in your home.

Break it down. Then build it up.

***

Here's some space to write down some household things you'd like to tackle during this season.

DAY 5

A time to weep,
And a time to laugh.
Ecclesiastes 3:4

Oh, laughing comes easily to me. I'm a bright-side girl. I diffuse every tense situation with a joke, sarcastic comment, *anything* to relieve the discomfort. To make someone chuckle gives me great relief.

Weeping, not so much. I'm usually surprised when I cry. A couple months ago, I walked into a fitting room at Macy's where Eric was helping our son Braden try on his wedding suit. I took one look at my little boy and burst into tears. I cry so rarely my boys all felt really sorry for me!

God created us with a wide range of emotions and ways to express them. It is *healthy* to find the emotional release that comes with both weeping and laughing. Maybe this is obvious and easy for you. It's not always for me.

Back in high school my friend Tammy found out her parents

were divorcing. As we talked about it, she said, "When I told Teresa," (our mutual friend), "She cried with me." I remember feeling vaguely guilty because I couldn't work up the emotion to empathize with Tammy's pain.

Rejoice with those who rejoice, and weep with those who weep. Romans 12:15 (NKJV)

There is a season for both.

It's often easier to shove down our pain and lean into laughter. I've heard the best comedians are the most broken inside. Robin Williams is a heartbreaking example of that. One of the great talents of our time, he had a deep well of internal struggle that never found its way out.

Take the time to feel, to cry, to express your pain, to fully experience your season of change or sadness. Don't just run faster or shove it down or keep busy or make jokes or throw out the ever-popular classic, "I'm fine."

Leading up to Braden's wedding, I told him I had a sneaking suspicion I was going to bawl. I even told his fiancée Alanah, "If I cry through the wedding, please know it's not about you. I really like you." Every time I thought of my dinosaur-loving, Hot-Wheels-playing little boy getting married, I choked up. I imagined myself watching his daddy perform the ceremony and indulging in a classy mother-of-the-groom cry from my seat down front.

But on the night of the wedding, I held it together because I needed to help host our guests and had to walk onstage to do the pastor-mom prayer of blessing during the ceremony. I didn't cry.

The following week was spent with my mother in town—shopping, massages, cooking and eating and chatting—and I started to think my opportunity to release my emotions was gone.

And then Aidan said we should watch the series finale of the show *The Middle*, where the parents say goodbye to their oldest son as he moves out of the state. And I burst into tears. Over a stupid TV show.

I cried.

I felt the pain of that season of motherhood right along with Patricia Heaton's character.

I looked over at Aidan and said, "What are you DOING to me? GAH! This is TERRIBLE!"

He looked back at me blankly and then said, "Oh. Because of Braden?"

And then we laughed.

A time to weep. A time to laugh.

There is a season for both. Don't skip your season.

***

Is there something you haven't mourned that you need to? Try journaling about it and expressing your emotions to God and/or a safe friend.

DAY 6

A time to mourn,
And a time to dance.
Ecclesiastes 3:4

A couple years ago a friend and partner in ministry walked out of my life. She wasn't upset with me, nor I her, but by her choice and God's leading, her season of doing life with me was done.

I was devastated. I'm in my 40's and have been in leadership for a long time now. I have learned to be OK with people leaving my church, therefore, leaving my life. People who were "all in" with us and our mission to reach people with the hope of Jesus, suddenly – or gradually – move on to what God has for them to do next.

But this one. This one broke my heart.

I mentioned yesterday that I don't cry much. That Saturday morning, I sobbed like a toddler who lost her doll. Eric held me, mentioned that he wasn't all that surprised (thanks, honey), and then we had to go to work.

29

The next night I called a friend from out of state. She's a pastor too, so she gets it. She listened to my story, shared a similar one, and then said some important words:

"I'll give you 48 hours to grieve, and then you need to get back to work."

Wow. Harsh. *Thanks, friend!*

But that's just it. There's a season to mourn. A *mourning period.* Take the time. Do the crying. Process the loss. And then *decide* to get back to your calling.

She said one other thing that I remember very clearly. "Pull your other girls close. Don't make them pay because one left you."

In other words, choose to lean in and live and love the ones who stay even though the other one walked away. Don't shut everyone out for fear of being rejected again. It'll happen, but you can't live in that fear. Choose to live fully anyway.

These pieces of wisdom came from a seasoned friend who's just a little ahead of me in life. They were so valuable, but hard to put into practice. Grieve 48 hours and then shake it off and get back to work? Keep my hurting heart open for my other girls to stay connected to the authentic *me* even though it's likely they won't all be there in a few years?

These choices require supernatural help. Fortunately, my God is a supernatural Father with a track record of mending broken hearts and allowing people to not only survive, but also to thrive in joy.

You have turned my mourning into joyful dancing. You have taken away my clothes of mourning and clothed me with joy...
Psalm 30:11 (NLT)

***

What relationship loss are you mourning or allowing to slide into bitterness or resentment?

_____

_____

Who are you making "pay" for your loss by not allowing them access to your authentic (whole) self?

_____

_____

Try handing this over to God today, praying something like this:

Dear God,

I have been mourning the loss of _____.
I ask You to please put an end to my season of mourning and heal my broken heart.

Don't let me withhold my full heart from _____
anymore, but rather let me love and live in joy with the relationships You have given me to keep for now.

Turn my mourning into smiling and dancing again, from the deepest parts of my soul, like only You can. And let me get back to work living out my calling from You.

Thank you.
In Jesus' name, amen.

DAY 7

A time to cast away stones,
And a time to gather stones.
Ecclesiastes 3:5

Several years ago, Eric and I went to Israel for the first time. As we toured the ancient sites that hold so much meaning for our Judeo-Christian faith, I made sure to pick up a small stone by which to remember each place. When we returned home, I lined a cigar box with mini-muffin cups. Labeling each cup, I set the stone inside as a remembrance of what I experienced in Israel.

On my dining room shelf is a large, flat stone we brought back from a family vacation in Idaho when the kiddos were little. We remember the fun we had on that vacation, especially the time a fish swam into Braden's shoe as he waded in a stream.

I wear a stone on my left ring finger that reminds me of Eric's love for me.

By our front door is a pile of stones, each engraved with a

family member's name. They were gifts from our neighbor at our last house. One of those family members doesn't live here anymore, but every time I see his stone, I see his face in my mind.

Holland has a stone in her room that we found at a coffee shop by Lake Michigan last summer. Someone had written *warm friends* on it. We wrote the name of the coffee shop on it and brought it home to remember that day.

In the Old Testament, it was common for God's people to stack some stones up at a place where God did something important or miraculous. That way, any time they passed by that place and saw those stones, they were reminded of God's hand at work in that season of their lives.

In the future your children will ask you, "What do these stones mean?" Then you can tell them, "They remind us that the Jordan River stopped flowing when the Ark of the Lord's Covenant went across." These stones will stand as a memorial among the people of Israel forever. Joshua 4:6-7 (NLT)

Remembrance stones keep a memory alive.

Today's verse says there's a season to gather stones and a season to cast them away. If we keep rolling with the stones-equal-memories concept, then gathering stones to commemorate good times is a cool idea.

But the verse says there is also a time to cast stones away. Some memories we should not re-hash. The painful ones, the negative words spoken over us, the betrayals, the traumatic events that left us scarred. What is it about those memories that draw us to pick them up, turn them over in our minds, and examine every surface of that remembrance stone?

Why keep those memories alive?

Sometimes I think it's because we feel like if we let them go, no one will hold the one who hurt us responsible. If we let them go, we have to give up trying to understand the *why*. If we cast the stone away, we are afraid we'll just be pretending it didn't affect us, but it really, really did.

Friend, God will hold those who hurt you responsible. Drop the stone.

You never will understand the *why*. There are not answers for everything, and that's good to recognize because thinking you can find all the answers is pretty heavy stone to carry in itself. Drop the stone.

Refusing to carry the stone doesn't mean the painful experience didn't affect you. You are not pretending it didn't happen; you just don't have to wake up every day and pick it up and relive it again. Cast the stone away.

You get to choose which stones you take with you on life's journey and which you cast away.

***

Today, maybe you can grab a marker and some stones and start writing. Then go find a lake or cliff or hole in the ground and cast those stones away for good.

Releasing the weight you're carrying will free you to pick up new stones, fresh memories, and much to be grateful for.

Beautiful days are ahead. Don't forget to gather the good stones along the way.

DAY 8

A time to embrace,
And a time to refrain from embracing.
Ecclesiastes 3:5

Oh, man. There's no way I can hear this verse without reliving a memory straight outta high school. For context, I went to a tiny Christian school that was run by my church in rural Alabama. It was *literally* in a cow field. My teacher was my principal and also my pastor. He went by Brother Lamar. He and his wife, Mrs. Pat, ran the school with tender hearts but lots of rules. The rules were super-strict. Dress code, language, music, behavior, boy-girl contact. Think *Footloose* with no redemption at the end.

So we were walking into class from the gym on the first day back from summer vacation, and my current crush, Tommy, and I stole a quick hug. Which was observed by Brother Lamar. Which prompted him to say, "Tommy! Kelly! There is a time to embrace, and a time to refrain from embracing."

I'm guessing it didn't embarrass Tommy at all, but I'm usually a rule-keeper. I was mortified and have remembered that moment to this day.

There's a time to embrace, and a time to refrain from embracing. There is a season to wrap your body around someone and give yourself fully to them physically. And there is a season to refrain.

Maybe you're referring to the above paragraphs and thinking I'm not qualified to talk to you about this because you're in a different world than the one I grew up in. HOWEVER, we are, right this minute, living in a world that has access to the Holy Word of God.

God, our Creator, wrote a Book by which we can see the wisest way to live according to His design for His children.

In this Book, these words are written:

Give honor to marriage, and remain faithful to one another in marriage. Hebrews 13:4 (NLT)

What is marriage? A lifelong covenant between two people.

'Til death do we part.
An in-front-of-God-and-everybody-that-matters solemn commitment to each other.
The real deal.
Not the promise or the intent or the expectation or the engagement ring.
The we-said-the-vows, stood-up-and-declared-on-an-actual-day *marriage*.

How do you honor marriage?

Don't jack with the covenant.

Don't pretend it's there when it's not. Don't ignore it when it is.

It is ONLY the covenant marriage relationship that wraps safe arms around the sexual experience. It says I'm completely vulnerable and connected to you and you alone, for my whole life.

Sex is literally the *only* thing that Scripture says should only be embraced in the covenant of marriage. We are called to honor that.

Anywhere, any way, that you take sex out of the covenant, you dishonor God's heart for you.

This is not my opinion. This is from God, your loving Creator's design for your best life. (See 1 Thessalonians 4:1-8)

There is a time to embrace—fully, completely, safely, wholly—*holy*—your sexuality. And there's a time to refrain.

Refrain outside the covenant. Inside? Hey. It's time to embrace. Go get it on!

***

A time to embrace, and a time to refrain from embracing.

In which season are you?

How can you honor marriage and stay faithful to yours (present or future)?

_____

_____

DAY 9

I mean, how can you read this without thinking about pounds on the scale?

A time to gain, and a time to lose.

If that didn't make you think about your weight, you probably have a healthy relationship with your body.

Whoop-de-doo, good for you.

Just kidding. I'm happy for you. Really.

My mom has long struggled with her weight, though in my mind she's never really been overweight. But this year she got going on a new healthy-living plan, and now my momma officially weighs less than me for the first time in my life. And she was quick to remind me that she's taller than me too. Hmph.

This has been bothering me, because it seems like the weight she managed to lose, I managed to *find*.

When she was in town for Braden's wedding, we were talking. She said, "You know, getting healthy and losing weight has just been my focus during this season of my life."

And honestly? When she said that, I felt curiously relieved and let myself off the hook a little bit.

See, I wanted to be thinner for the wedding pictures. I wanted to be looking and feeling fabulous as the mother of the groom. Instead, I weigh the most I have *ever* weighed unpregnant.

And I felt a little crappy about it. WHY, oh why didn't I put in the work and the self-discipline to slim down instead of lump it on? Why didn't I hit the gym more and eat bread less and say yes to crunches and no to dessert?

Because it was not my season to focus on that. And that's ok.

There's a time to gain, and a time to lose.

You may have the opposite problem. Your size issues may propel you to an unhealthy deprivation of what your body needs: rest, calories, grace, approval.

There's a time to gain, and a time to lose.

It's not always my season to focus on weight loss. It's ok. I'm going to trust that God will give me the want-to and the ability to focus for real on it during the right season.

In the meantime, I'm doing the best I can. I ask Him for wisdom.

I decline the obviously unhealthy and try to take time to listen to my body and give it what it needs.

This is my season at the moment.

Go easy on yourself, OK?

Take care of your body, but don't be hard on yourself when you don't measure up to your ideal measurements. Your body has accomplished a lot. You are strong. You are beautiful exactly as you are, in this moment.

When God thinks of you, His eyes twinkle. He does not care about your cellulite or saggy boobs. Imagine God obsessing about the things about your body that you obsess about. That'll give you a chuckle. You know He doesn't judge you one tiny bit about that stuff.

Maybe soon your season will change. For now, embrace where you are and do the best you can.

Thank you for making me so wonderfully complex! Your workmanship is marvelous—how well I know it. Psalm 139:14 (NLT)

***

Which season are you in right now?

What can you do during this season to care well for your body?

DAY 10

A time to keep,
And a time to throw away.
Ecclesiastes 3:6

One of the defining characteristics typical of women is the nesting instinct, which compels us to surround ourselves with things that provide comfort, ease of living, and a sense of ownership in our place.

The things we need in order to feel "at home" vary with our uniqueness.

Fluffy throw pillows
An electric toothbrush
A pot or pan for every recipe
A deep freezer
Shoes for every occasion
Hair styling tools, products, and accessories

Then there are the things that hold memories.

Sports jerseys
Ticket stubs
Baby clothes & furniture
Vacation souvenirs
Formal dresses

And the things we keep in case we need/want them someday.

Books
Décor
Kitchen tools
Jewelry
Lotions, creams, perfumes

Truth is, the things we require for a happy, supplied life change with our seasons. Except we tend to keep it all. Because you never know when you might wish you had it.

There's a time to keep, and a time to throw away.

Keep when it brings you true joy, functionality, pleasure, beauty.

Throw away when it becomes soul-sucking clutter, you no longer need it, or when you look at it, your heart doesn't smile.

Take a picture of that bridesmaid's dress and then donate it to Goodwill so some high school girl can wear it to an ugly-dress-party. (Kidding. Sorta.)

If you've been married 20 years and haven't used the food processor Aunt Gertie gave you, say Bye, Felicia.

You will probably never use that perfume sample your Mary-Kay-rep mother gave you. (Remind me to delete this before it goes to print so my mom doesn't see it.)

If one day you find yourself truly *needing* something you've thrown out, God will provide. He *always* provides for His kids.

And this same God who takes care of me will supply all your needs from his glorious riches, which have been given to us in Christ Jesus. Philippians 4:19 (NLT)

You get the point. Our security is not in our stuff. It's in our good Father who cares for us. He doesn't want you drowning in clutter and stuff you *think* will make you happy but instead makes you have more junk to dust.

A time to keep.

A time to throw away.

Throw away season starts today! Go!

DAY 11

A time to tear,
And a time to sew.
Ecclesiastes 3:7

The *New Living Translation* phrases it, "A time to tear and a time to mend." Which made me think about mending relationships.

> Since God chose you to be the holy people he loves, you must clothe yourselves with tenderhearted mercy, kindness, humility, gentleness, and patience. Make allowance for each other's faults, and forgive anyone who offends you. Remember, the Lord forgave you, so you must forgive others. Above all, clothe yourselves with love, which binds us all together in perfect harmony. And let the peace that comes from Christ rule in your hearts. *Colossians 3:12-15 (NLT)*

God's heart is for His people to have healthy relationships. But the truth of life's seasons is that not all relationships are tight forever. So. How does that work?

Well, there's a time to mend relationships: when they are broken in a way that needs forgiveness and grace to bring the mending and healing.

And there's a time to tear relationships apart. Not a violent tearing, but a gentle, careful separation, kind of like when you are separating an important paper at the perforation.

Friendships are for *reasons* and *seasons*. A couple years ago, I met a woman in the elevator of our apartment building in St. Paul. Her name was Diane, and I learned that she was a spiritual director, which is kind of a cross between pastor and counselor. We exchanged phone numbers, and about four months later, I needed someone to talk to.

We met a few times over a few months, and then we were done. When we moved from the building, I never even went upstairs to say goodbye. We were friends for a reason in my life. I know if I called her tomorrow, she would be there for me again.

Others are friends for a season – like the friend I mentioned on Day 6. Her season with me helped shape the way I saw my role in the world and the needs of the women around me. I am grateful for the season we spent together, even though the tearing away was painful. And I know that if our paths cross again at any point, we will always have a harmony that comes from being sisters in Christ.

When we are able, it is always God's heart that we mend broken relationships where we have done wrong or been wronged.

But we also need to be OK with the tearing away; a loving, grace-filled separation that happens naturally as we each pursue the life God has for us.

***

Work it out a bit: What broken relationship do you know you need to do your part in mending?

_____

_____

Take a step: Reach out. Apologize. Forgive. Ask for wisdom from a godly person if you need to first.

What "torn away" relationship do you need to release, knowing its season is over?

_____

_____

Take a step (if God leads you): Write a note that says how grateful you are for the friendship, the help, and the season you had together. If it's appropriate, mail the note. If not, maybe the note was just an exercise for your heart. Just tear it up and let it go.

DAY 12

A time to keep silence,
And a time to speak.
Ecclesiastes 3:7

This one is Sooooo Easy for me.

Ha.

It's pretty straightforward. What else is there to say?

There's a time to talk and a time to shut it. Most of us wish we were better at taming our tongues. We know we should, blah blah blah.

So today I'm going to talk for just a second about venting and releasing.

You know how it goes. Someone does something that just torques you, and you *just need to vent for a minute*. So you find a friend or sympathetic/captive listener and cut loose. Those of us who are God-followers often feel a little guilty about indulging in the gripe-fest, but we excuse it with the words, "OK, I'm letting it go, I'm fine now. I forgive her. I just needed to vent."

But here's what venting does:

It gives voice to angry, unloving (and possibly ungodly) thoughts.
It brings another person into a situation that was between you and someone else, making it a form of gossip.
It can cause your listener to hold a grudge against the person you're venting about.
It puts focus on negativity.

Here's what venting does not do:

It does not honor God, because He tells us to set our mind on things that are good, pure, lovely, etc.

Fix your thoughts on what is true, and honorable, and right, and pure, and lovely, and admirable. Think about things that are excellent and worthy of praise. Philippians 4:8 (NLT)

It does not build anyone up.

So encourage each other and build each other up, just as you are already doing. 1 Thessalonians 5:11 (NLT)

Great. So we shouldn't vent. Then how do we deal with the buildup of pressure that comes with an unfortunate situation?

Don't vent. *Release.*

Believe it or not, God is capable of taking your big bubble of frustration and letting the air right out of it. IF you remember to involve Him before involving your tongue.

Inhale deeply, and on your exhale, release your anger to God. Like, really give it to Him.

God, I am SO FRUSTRATED. That wasn't fair. I shouldn't have been treated that way. I wanna punch somebody...

Whatever you're dealing with, God can handle it. Don't vent to a person. Release it to God. Then ask Him for what you need.

Help me know how to deal with this. Help me forgive that person. Help me know what to say to them to get it worked out.

Understand this, my dear brothers and sisters: You must all be quick to listen, slow to speak, and slow to get angry. James 1:19 (NLT)

Honestly, the only way to pull that off is to decide NOW that the next time you're tempted to vent, you'll submit to that very quiet voice of the Holy Spirit in you that says, *release it to me.*

A time to keep silence, and a time to speak.

Only speak when you have released your frustration to God and can graciously have the conversation you need to have.

DAY 13

A time to love,
And a time to hate.
Ecclesiastes 3:8

Jesus replied, "You must love the LORD your God with all your heart, all your soul, and all your mind. This is the first and greatest commandment. A second is equally important: Love your neighbor as yourself." Matthew 22:37-39 (NLT)

There is a time to love; and from the words of Jesus, it would appear that there's no room to hate anyone, ever. True story. There's no room to hate people.

So when is it a time to hate?

We hate what opposes God.

You who love the Lord, hate evil! Psalm 97:10 (NKJV)

Abhor what is evil. Cling to what is good. Romans 12:9 (NKJV)

Abhor. Fancy word.

Dictionary.com defines *abhor* this way: *to regard with extreme repugnance or aversion; detest utterly; loathe; abominate.*

Whatever goes against God—who is pure love, pure good—is evil.

You cannot fully love God and also love indulging in thoughts and behaviors that go against His heart for you. Those things are called sin.

Sin: anything that goes against God's heart and guide for your life.

There is a time to love. Love God, who created you, knows you intimately, and wants to be in relationship with you so much that Jesus gave His life to secure your forgiveness for your sins that separated you from God.

There is a time to hate. Hate the sin, the evil that sneaks in and causes you to miss God's best for you. Hate what rises up in direct defiance to the good the Holy Spirit seeks to grow in your life.

Here's a question for you to consider today: *How much* do you hate your sin?

I could give you a sample list of sins here, but I'm not going to.

Instead, stop right here for a minute and courageously, out loud, pray this prayer to God:

Search me, O God, and know my heart; test me and know my anxious thoughts. Point out anything in me that offends you,

and lead me along the path of everlasting life.
Psalm 139:23-24 (NLT)

Ask Him to convict your heart of the sin that is causing you to miss His best for you. What comes to your mind? Really take time to listen to the Holy Spirit gently nudging your heart.

Do you have the courage to write it down and confess it to God and ask forgiveness? Ask Him to help you *detest* what grieves His heart.

_____

_____

_____

_____

_____

_____

_____

If we say that we have no sin, we deceive ourselves, and the truth is not in us. If we confess our sins, He is faithful and just to forgive us our sins and to cleanse us from all unrighteousness.
1 John 1:8-9 (NKJV)

Girl, there is no condemnation here. There is only a passionate plea to *please* let God clean up the broken parts and cause you to wholeheartedly love Him and let Him lead you forward.

It starts by loving God. And hating anything that gets between you.

A time to love. A time to hate.

DAY 14

A time of war,
And a time of peace.
Ecclesiastes 3:8

You are a warrior. Each day you put on your war paint and do battle as you go through this crazy, multi-seasoned journey called life.

You cannot avoid the fight.

The fight to get through each day.
The fight to earn income and pay bills.
The fight to raise your kids right.
To love your loved ones unselfishly.
To see the right decisions in the midst of many options.
To actually do the right things.
To keep your temper when others don't.
To endure personal pain and keep going.
To push back darkness and shine the light of Jesus.

There is a time of war – to fight the daily battles.

And there is a time of peace.

Mostly, we know war way better than peace.

The war, as I said, is unavoidable. It ensures your survival.

Peace is a choice you must make. It ensures your sanity.

We snatch seasons of peace by way of vacations and holidays, but those are few and have way too much war between.

My challenge to you today: don't only seek peace as reprieve from the war. Seek peace *before you go* to war. In other words, engage the fight from a place of peace.

Get your little shot of peace and inner stillness each day before you go to war. Don't just hit your alarm, roll out of bed, and start the day without equipping yourself for the battles you will face.

God has armor for you. Don't leave it hanging in the closet when you walk out your door.

> *And that about wraps it up. God is strong, and he wants you strong. So take everything the Master has set out for you, well-made weapons of the best materials. And put them to use so you will be able to stand up to everything the Devil throws your way.*
>
> *This is no afternoon athletic contest that we'll walk away from and forget about in a couple of hours. This is for keeps, a life-or-death fight to the finish against the Devil and all his angels.*

Be prepared. You're up against far more than you can handle on your own. Take all the help you can get, every weapon God has issued, so that when it's all over but the shouting you'll still be on your feet.

Truth, righteousness, peace, faith, and salvation are more than words. Learn how to apply them. You'll need them throughout your life.

God's Word is an indispensable weapon. In the same way, prayer is essential in this ongoing warfare. Pray hard and long. Pray for your brothers and sisters.

Keep your eyes open. Keep each other's spirits up so that no one falls behind or drops out. Ephesians 6:10-18 (MSG)

Aaaah, so many empowering words there. The struggle is real, but you have the weapons, resources, inspiration, and supernatural power to win. Use them. Remind yourself each morning that the victory is already yours through Christ Jesus, and His Spirit guiding you. Start each day finding His peace, and then go to war.

Don't worry about anything; instead, pray about everything. Tell God what you need, and thank him for all he has done. Then you will experience God's peace, which exceeds anything we can understand. His peace will guard your hearts and minds as you live in Christ Jesus. Philippians 4:6-7 (NLT)

CONCLUSION

He has made everything beautiful in its time.

Also He has put eternity in their hearts,
except that no one can find out the work that
God does from beginning to end.

I know that nothing is better for them than to rejoice,
and to do good in their lives,

And also that every man should eat and drink and
enjoy the good of all his labor—it is the gift of God.

Ecclesiastes 3:9-13 (NKJV)

You may be loving this season, or it may be the hardest one of your life so far. Here's what I know: you can choose to believe God is working on something beautiful that you can't see, or you can despair that it will never get better. It's a choice you make.

In the meantime, seek the peace of God in your heart. Lean in close and get to know Him better. Do the work that is in front of you. Find moments of joy, and receive with gratitude the small gifts He has all around you.

One day you'll look back and realize the season has passed and you're in a new one.

Seasons are sneaky that way.

And God is always faithful.

ABOUT THE AUTHOR

Kelly Dykstra used to think she was just along for the ride in life, but then God empowered her stand on her own two feet (usually in sweet high heels) and go after her own destiny. She's passionate about freeing other women up to do the same.

Kelly and her husband Eric co-founded The Crossing, a multi-site church based near Minneapolis, in 2004. You can find their ministry online at freegrace.tv.

Her other books include *How to Twirl: A Lovely Way to Live* and *The People Mover: The Secret to Effortless Faith* (both available from Amazon or The Crossing Church).

Her favorite things (in no particular order) include Heinz Genuine Dill Pickles, home decorating, cooking for her family (kiddos Holland, Aidan, Braden & his wife Alanah), massages, traveling, and date nights with Eric.

Made in the USA
Lexington, KY
03 July 2018